ES6 and JS

Learn ECMASCRIPT 6 quickly

Quick ES2015 Scripting With Babel.js

Sandeep Kumar Patel

Quick ES2015 Scripting Using Babel.js

Published By

Sandeep Kumar Patel.

Table of Content

1

Configuring Babel

Babel is a JavaScript compiler which enable developers to work with new JavaScript features provided by ECMAScript. Babel is a compiler that takes ES6 and compiles it down to regular Javascript that runs in your browser.

> *The Babel source code can be found in the following Github link:-*
> *https://github.com/babel/babel*
>
> *The gulp-babel module can be found in the following Github link:-*
> *https://www.npmjs.com/package/gulp-babel*

Babel has wide variety of Plugin supports for automating compilation of futuristic code to the currently supported javascript. In this chapter we will learn to install and configure Babel compiler with Gulp build system.

Configuring Gulp with Babel

To Demonstrate ES6 features with Babel we have created **ES6FeatureDemo** project. The **ES6FeatureDemo** directory will contain all our example code. We can use **gulp-babel** plugin to create Gulp task to automate Babel transpiration. We need to install Gulp module before proceeding in the demo. Gulp module can be installed using **npm install gulp --save-dev** command. The following screenshot shows the terminal with Gulp installation: -

```
Terminal                                                                    ⚙ ⬇
+ J:\ES6FeatureDemo>npm install gulp --save-dev
✗ npm WARN package.json es6-feature-demo@1.0.0 No description
  npm WARN package.json es6-feature-demo@1.0.0 No repository fi
  eld.
  npm WARN package.json es6-feature-demo@1.0.0 No README data
  gulp@3.9.0 node_modules\gulp
  ├── pretty-hrtime@1.0.1
  ├── interpret@0.6.6
  ├── deprecated@0.0.1
  ├── archy@1.0.0
```

Babel module can be installed using **npm install gulp-babel --save-dev** command. The
following screenshot shows the terminal with gulp-babel installation: -

```
Terminal                                                                    ⚙ ⬇
+ J:\ES6FeatureDemo>npm install gulp-babel --save-dev
✗ npm WARN package.json es6-feature-demo@1.0.0 No description
  npm WARN package.json es6-feature-demo@1.0.0 No repository fi
  eld.
  npm WARN package.json es6-feature-demo@1.0.0 No README data
  gulp-babel@5.3.0 node_modules\gulp-babel
  ├── object-assign@4.0.1
  ├── replace-ext@0.0.1
  ├── through2@2.0.0 (xtend@4.0.0, readable-stream@2.0.2)
  ├── gulp-util@3.0.7 (array-differ@1.0.0, array-uniq@1.0.2, fa
```

Project structure

On successful installation of all dependencies the project **ES6FeatureDemo** looks like
following screenshot: -

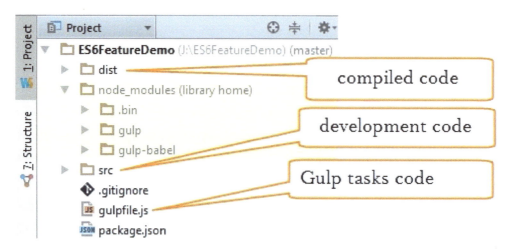

The details of **ES6FeatureDemo** project screenshot is as follows: -

- **ES6FeatureDemo** has 2 new directory **src** and **dist.** The **src** directory contains all the development code prior to Babel transpilation. The **dist** directory contains the Babel generated transpiled code.

- The **gulpfile.js** contains the code definition of Gulp tasks for Babel transpilation.

Defining Gulp task

The **gulpfile.js** has code definition for 3 gulp tasks **babel**, **babel:watch** and **default**. The code content of **gulpfile.js** are as follows: -

```javascript
var gulp = require('gulp'),
    babel = require('gulp-babel');
gulp.task('babel', function () {
    return gulp.src('src/**/*.js')
        .pipe(babel({optional: ['runtime']}))
        .pipe(gulp.dest('dist'));
});
gulp.task('babel:watch', function () {
    return gulp.watch('src/**/*.js',['babel'])
});
gulp.task('default',['babel', 'babel:watch'] );
```

The details of these 3 tasks are as follows: -

- The **babel** task loads the javascript file present in the **src** directory and pipes it to Babel **runtime** to generate compiled code and then it pipes it to **dest** directory where the converted code will be saved.

- The **babel:watch** task monitors the **src/**/*.js** files and for any change in the javascript code it calls the **babel** task to generate transpiled code and saves it to **dest** directory.

- The **default** task is a combination of **babel** and **babel:watch** task.

We can find all the Gulp tasks are listed in the Gulp console in the WebStorm editor. The following screenshot shows the WebStorm Gulp console listed all the tasks: -

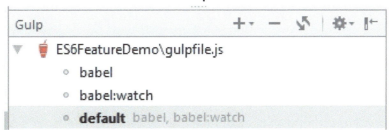

Summary

In this chapter we have learnt about Babel compiler and learn to setup Gulp build system to create task that tarnspile next generation javascript code to currently supported javascript. In the coming chapter we will start to explore the new features provided by ES6.

2

Spread Operator

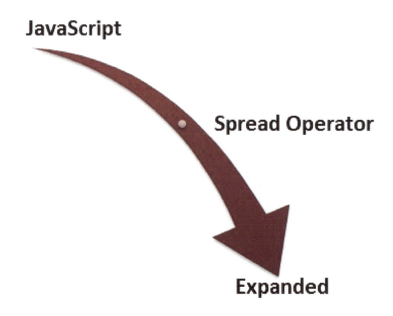

In the previous chapter we have learnt to install and configure **gulp-babel** plugin. We have also developed Gulp tasks in gulpfile.js which will transpile the development version of javascript to supported JavaScript code. In this chapter we will learn to use spread operator.

Implementing Spread Operator

The **spread operator** allows an expression to be expanded in places where multiple arguments are expected. A spread operator is represented by **3 dots (...)**. A spread operator expression can be declared by prefixing **3 dot (...)** operator before the variable name.

In previous chapter we have creates a **ES6FeatureDemo** project to write all the code for this book. To understand spread operator, we have created all the example file in **src/spread_operator** directory. The transpiled code by Babel will be present in **dist/spread_operator** directory. The updated directory structure looks like following screenshot: -

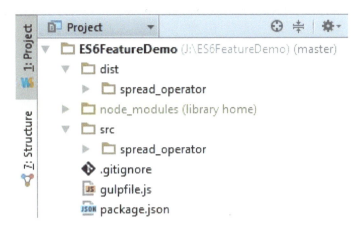

Example: Array expansion using spread operator

The 1st example on spread operator implementation is present in **src/ spread_operator /example1.js** file. The code content of **src/spread_operator/example1.js** are as follows: -

```javascript
//Array expansion using spread operator
var mathStudents = ["Sandeep", "Sangeeta", "Surabhi"],
    lawStudents = ["Sumanta", "Rohan", "Surendra"],
    allStudents= ["John", ...mathStudents, "Jack",...lawStudents];
console.log(allStudents);
```

In the previous code we have 3 arrays of student name. The **mathStudents** array contains 3 names of mathematic student. The **lawStudents** array contains 3 names of Law students. The **allStudents** array contains 2 student names **John**, **Jack** and **2 spread** variable **...mathStudents**, **...lawStudents**.

Now we can run the Gulp default task to transpile the **src/ spread_operator/example1.js** file. To start the transpilation use **Gulp** command. The following screenshot shows the terminal with Gulp task in execution and watcher is indefinite loop to monitor the change in code: -

```
Terminal                                                          ⚙ ⭷ ⌄ ↧
+ J:\ES6FeatureDemo>gulp
✕ [12:07:59] Using gulpfile J:\ES6FeatureDemo\gulpfile.js
  [12:07:59] Starting 'babel'...
  [12:07:59] Starting 'babel:watch'...
  [12:07:59] Finished 'babel:watch' after 15 ms
  [12:07:59] Finished 'babel' after 179 ms
  [12:07:59] Starting 'default'...
  [12:07:59] Finished 'default' after 33 µs
```

The transpiled code by Babel will be available in **dist/ spread_operator/example1.js** file. The code content of **dist/spread_operator/example1.js** file are as follows: -

```
//Array expansion using spread operator
"use strict";
var mathStudents = ["Sandeep", "Sangeeta", "Surabhi"],
   lawStudents = ["Sumanta", "Rohan", "Surendra"],
   allStudents = ["John"].concat(mathStudents, ["Jack"], lawStudents);
console.log(allStudents);
```

The previous code is **babelified** code and we can clearly identify that the spread operator expansion logic is achieved using **concat()** method which is a member method of Array object wand supported by present JavaScript version. The following screenshot shows the updated directory structure of **ES6FeatureDemo** project: -

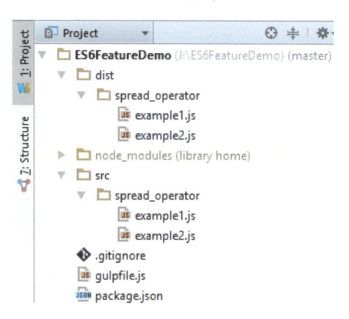

Now we can run **dist/spread_operator/example1.js** code using **node dist/spread_operator/example1.js** command. The following screenshot shows the terminal with node execution and output in terminal: -

```
Terminal
J:\ES6FeatureDemo>node dist/spread_operator/example1.js
[ 'John',
  'Sandeep',
  'Sangeeta',
  'Surabhi',
  'Jack',
  'Sumanta',
  'Rohan',
  'Surendra' ]

J:\ES6FeatureDemo>
```

Example: Multiple Arguments

The 2nd example on spread operator implementation is present in **src/example2.js** file. The code content of **src/example2.js** are as follows: -

```javascript
//multiple input parameter using spread operator
var numberArray1 = [12,21,32,40];
var numberArray2 = [10,22,30];
var summation = function(...items){
  var sum = 0;
  items.forEach(function(item) {
    sum = sum+item;
  });
  return sum;
};
var result1 = summation(...numberArray1);
console.log("Result1: ",result1);
var result2 = summation(...numberArray2);
console.log("Result2: ",result2);
```

In the previous code we have a method named **summation()** which takes a spread array element and iterates over the elements and returns the addition as a result. Due to the use of the spread operator the **summation()** method can handle any number of argument passed. Now we can run the Gulp task using **gulp** command. The following screenshot shows the terminal with gulp task execution: -

```
Terminal                                                              ⚙ ⬇

+  J:\ES6FeatureDemo>gulp
✕  [22:04:40] Using gulpfile J:\ES6FeatureDemo\gulpfile.js
   [22:04:40] Starting 'babel'...
   [22:04:40] Starting 'babel:watch'...
   [22:04:40] Finished 'babel:watch' after 14 ms
   [22:04:41] Finished 'babel' after 192 ms
   [22:04:41] Starting 'default'...
   [22:04:41] Finished 'default' after 19 µs
```

The transpiled code is available in the **dist/spread_operator/example2.js** file. The code content of **dist/spread_operator/example2.js** is as follows: -

```javascript
//multiple input parameter using spread operator
"use strict";
var numberArray1 = [12, 21, 32, 40];
var numberArray2 = [10, 22, 30];
var summation = function summation() {
```

```javascript
      var sum = 0;
      for (var _len = arguments.length, items = Array(_len),
      _key = 0; _key < _len; _key++) {
        items[_key] = arguments[_key];
      }
      items.forEach(function (item) {
        sum = sum + item;
      });
      return sum;
    };
    var result1 = summation.apply(undefined, numberArray1);
    console.log("Result1: ", result1);
    var result2 = summation.apply(undefined, numberArray2);
    console.log("Result2: ", result2);
```

From the previous code we can observe that Babel has compiled the code to generate the supported javascript code. Now we can run **dist/spread_operator/example2.js** code using **node dist/spread_operator/example2.js** command. The following screenshot shows the terminal with node execution and output in terminal: -

```
Terminal                                                          ✿ ⁃ ⌄

+  J:\ES6FeatureDemo>node dist/spread_operator/example2.js
✗  Result1:   105
   Result2:   62

   J:\ES6FeatureDemo>
```

Summary

In this chapter we have learnt about spread operator with coded example. In the next chapter we will learn more ES6 features. Till then stay tuned.

Arrow Operator

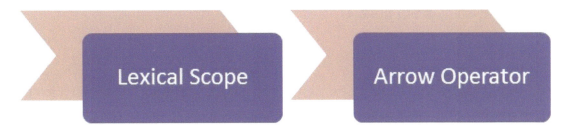

In the previous chapter we have learnt about spread operator. We have also developed some example to understand the use of Spread operator. In this chapter we will learn to use arrow operator.

Implementing Arrow Operator

An arrow operator is also named as **fat arrow** operator. An operator is represent using **imply (=>)** symbol. We should not be compare arrow operator to a normal javascript **function** keyword. Arrow operator are used for defining **lexical** scoping. The updated project **ES6FeatureDemo** structure look like following screenshot: -

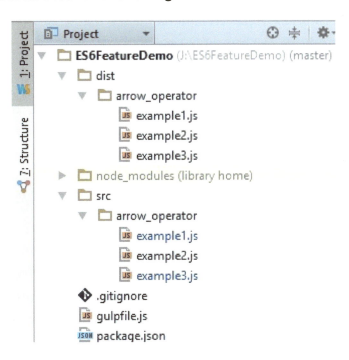

We have created an **arrow_operator** directory inside **src** folder to demonstrate use of arrow operator. The compiled code produced by Gulp task is present in **dist** folder in respective example files. Now we can develop some example using arrow operator.

Example: Function Call Using Arrow Operator

The **src/arrow_operator/example1.js** file contains the code define a method using Arrow operator. The code content of **src/arrow_operator/example1.js** file are as follows: -

```
//Function Call Using Arrow Operator
var sayHello = (name) =>{
   console.log("Hello ",name);
};
sayHello("Sandeep");
```

In the previous code we have developed a method named **sayHello()** method which takes a input parameter and prints it in the console message. Now we can run the **gulp** task to generate the babelified code. The code content of **dist/arrow_operator/example1.js** file are as follows: -

```
//Function Call With Arrow Operator
"use strict";
var sayHello = function sayHello(name) {
   console.log("Hello ", name);
};
sayHello("Sandeep");
```

From the previous code we can observe that Babel has compiled the code to generate the supported javascript code. Now we can run **dist/arrow_operator/example1.js** code using **node dist/arrow_operator/example1.js** command. The following screenshot shows the terminal with node execution and output in terminal: -

```
Terminal                                                    ⚙ ⋅ ⬇

+ J:\ES6FeatureDemo>node dist/arrow_operator/example1.js
✗ Hello   Sandeep

  J:\ES6FeatureDemo>█
```

Example: Map function with Arrow operator

The **src/arrow_operator/example2.js** file contains the code to use arrow operator in **map()** function. The code content of **src/arrow_operator/example2.js** file are as follows: -

```
// Map function With Arrow operator
var numbers = [1,2,3,4,5];
var result = numbers.map((number) => number * 2);
console.log("Result: ",result);
```

In the previous code we have a number array named **numbers**. The **map()** function is used to iterate over the elements and pass it to processing code block using arrow operator. The processing block referred by arrow operator takes each element and **multiply it with 2** and prints the result in console. Now we can run the **gulp** task to generate the babelified code. The code content of **dist/arrow_operator/example2.js** file are as follows: -

```
// Map function With Arrow operator
"use strict";
var numbers = [1, 2, 3, 4, 5];
var result = numbers.map(function (number) {
  return number * 2;
});
console.log("Result: ", result);
```

From the previous code we can observe that Babel has compiled the code to generate the supported javascript code. Now we can run **dist/arrow_operator/example2.js** code using **node dist/arrow_operator/example2.js** command. The following screenshot shows the terminal with node execution and output in terminal: -

```
Terminal                                              ⚙ ⭳
+  J:\ES6FeatureDemo>node dist/arrow_operator/example2.js
✕
   Result:  [ 2, 4, 6, 8, 10 ]

   J:\ES6FeatureDemo>█
```

Example: ForEach loop with Arrow operator

The **src/arrow_operator/example3.js** file contains the code to use arrow operator in **forEach()** function. The code content of **src/arrow_operator/example3.js** file are as follows:-

```
//ForEach loop with Arrow operator
var numbers = [1,2,3,4,5];
numbers.forEach(number => {
   console.log("Result: ",number*number);
});
```

In the previous code we have a number array named **numbers**. The **forEach()** function is used to iterate over the elements and pass it to processing code block using arrow operator. The processing block referred by arrow operator takes each element and **finds square** and prints the result in console. Now we can run the **gulp** task to generate the babelified code. The code content of **dist/arrow_operator/example3.js** file are as follows: -

```javascript
//ForEach with Arrow operator
"use strict";
var numbers = [1, 2, 3, 4, 5];
numbers.forEach(function (number) {
    console.log("Result: ", number * number);
});
```

From the previous code we can observe that Babel has compiled the code to generate the supported javascript code. Now we can run **dist/arrow_operator/example3.js** code using **node dist/arrow_operator/example3.js** command. The following screenshot shows the terminal with node execution and output in terminal: -

```
Terminal                                               ⚙ ⬇
 +  J:\ES6FeatureDemo>node dist/arrow_operator/example3.js
 ✕
    Result:   1
    Result:   4
    Result:   9
    Result:   16
    Result:   25

    J:\ES6FeatureDemo>
```

Summary

In this chapter we have learnt about arrow operator with coded example. In the next chapter we will learn more ES6 features. Till then stay tuned.

Block Scope with let keyword

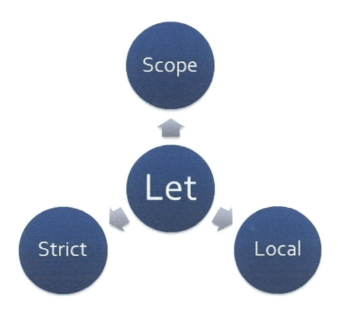

In the previous chapter we have learnt about arrow operator. We have also developed some example to understand the use of arrow operator. In this chapter we will learn to use Let keyword.

Implementing Let Keyword

ES6 provides the true **block** scope binding using **Let** keyword. Let allows us to declare variables that are limited in scope to the block, statement, or expression on which it is used. variable declared in **var** keyword are global or local to an entire function regardless of block scope. The updated project **ES6FeatureDemo** structure look like following screenshot: -

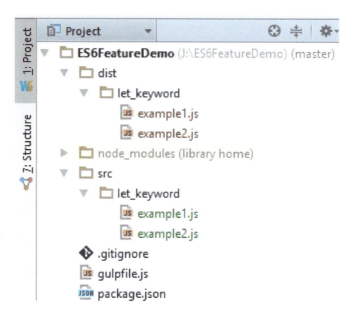

We have created a **let_keyword** directory inside **src** folder to demonstrate use of Let keyword. The compiled code produced by Gulp task is present in **dist** folder in respective example files. Now we can develop some example using Let keyword.

Example: Defining Variable using Let

The **src/let_keyword/example1.js** file contains the code define a variable using Let keyword. The code content of **src/let_keyword/example1.js** file are as follows: -

```
//Assigning value to variable
let number1 = 6;
console.log("number1: ", number1);
```

In the previous code we have declared a variable named **number1**. Now we can run the **gulp** task to generate the babelified code. The code content of **dist/ let_keyword /example1.js** file are as follows: -

```
//Assigning value to variable
"use strict";
var number1 = 6;
console.log("number1: ", number1);
```

From the previous code we can observe that Babel has compiled the code to generate the supported javascript code. Now we can run **dist/ let_keyword /example1.js** code using **node dist/ let_keyword /example1.js** command. The following screenshot shows the terminal with node execution and output in terminal: -

Example: Difference between Var and Let

The **src/let_keyword/example2.js** file contains the code to use Let keyword in **map()** function. The code content of **src/let_keyword /example2.js** file are as follows: -

```javascript
//scoping difference between var and let
var doSomeWork = function(){
  var number1 = 5;
  let number2 = 7;
  if(number1 >1){
    console.log("number1 "+number1);
    console.log("number2 "+number2);
    var number3 = 5;
    let number4 = 7;
  }
  console.log("number3 "+number3);
  console.log("number4 "+number4);
};
doSomeWork();
```

In the previous code we have a method named **doSomeWork()** method. The **number3** variable is defined using **var** keyword and **number4** is defined using **Let** keyword. Now we can run the gulp **task** to generate the babelified code. The content of **dist/let_keyword/example2.js** file are as follows: -

```javascript
//scoping difference between var and let
"use strict";
var doSomeWork = function doSomeWork() {
  var number1 = 5;
  var number2 = 7;
  if (number1 > 1) {
    console.log("number1 " + number1);
    console.log("number2 " + number2);
    var number3 = 5;
    var _number4 = 7;
  }
  console.log("number3 " + number3);
  console.log("number4 " + number4);
};
doSomeWork();
```

From the previous code we can observe that Babel has compiled the code to generate the supported javascript code. Now we can run **dist/ let_keyword /example2.js** code using **node dist/ let_keyword /example2.js** command. As **number4** is declared using **Let** keyword and hence we can see **ReferenceError** for **number4 is not defined**. This shows the Let provides the pure scope which makes the number4 is present only inside the scope of if statement. The following screenshot shows the terminal with node execution and output in terminal: -

```
Terminal                                                    ☼ ▾  ±

+  J:\ES6FeatureDemo\dist\let_keyword\example2.js:14
✗      console.log("number4 " + number4);
                               ^


   ReferenceError: number4 is not defined
       at doSomeWork (J:\ES6FeatureDemo\dist\let_keyword\example2.js
   :14:30)
       at Object.<anonymous> (J:\ES6FeatureDemo\dist\let_keyword\exa
   mple2.js:16:1)
       at Module._compile (module.js:434:26)
       at Object.Module._extensions..js (module.js:452:10)
       at Module.load (module.js:355:32)
       at Function.Module._load (module.js:310:12)
       at Function.Module.runMain (module.js:475:10)
       at startup (node.js:117:18)
       at node.js:951:3

   J:\ES6FeatureDemo>
```

Summary

In this chapter we have learnt about Let keyword with coded example. In the next chapter we will learn more ES6 features. Till then stay tuned.

Parameter with Default Value

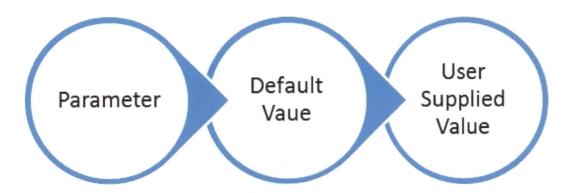

In the previous chapter we have learnt about let keyword. In this chapter we will learn about function parameters and initializing them with default values.

Implementing Default Value

ES6 provides a feature for passing **default values** of input parameters. The default value of a parameter can be configured using **Assignment Parameter (=).** The updated project **ES6FeatureDemo** structure look like following screenshot: -

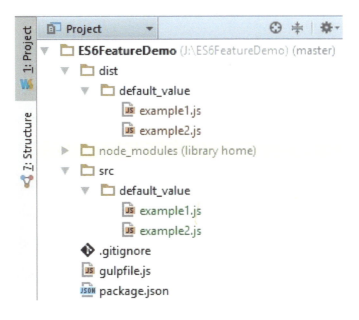

We have created a **default_value** directory inside **src** folder to demonstrate default value of parameter. The compiled code produced by Gulp task is present in **dist** folder in respective example files. Now we can develop some example to demonstrate default values of parameters.

Example: Function Parameter Default Value

The **src/default_value/example1.js** file contains the code for defining a method with default values for the mentioned parameters. The code content of **src/default_value/example1.js** file are as follows: -

```
//Function parameter default value
var multiplyTwoNumbers = function(number1, number2 = 1){
  return number1*number2;
};
var result = multiplyTwoNumbers(5);
console.log("Result: ",result);
```

In the previous code we have declared a method **multiplyTwoNumbers()** with 2 parameters **number1** and **number2**.The **default** value assigned to **number2** is 1.It means if the user forgot to supply any value for **number2** parameter then it is considered **1** is the value **number2** parameter. Now we can run the **gulp** task to generate the babelified code. The code content of **dist/default_value /example1.js** file are as follows: -

```
//Function parameter default value
"use strict";
var multiplyTwoNumbers = function multiplyTwoNumbers(number1) {
  var number2 = arguments.length <= 1 || arguments[1] === undefined ? 1 : arguments[1];
  return number1 * number2;
};
var result = multiplyTwoNumbers(5);
console.log("Result: ", result);
```

From the previous code we can observe that Babel has compiled the code to generate the supported javascript code. Now we can run **dist/default_value/example1.js** code using **node dist/default_value/example1.js** command. The following screenshot shows the terminal with node execution and output in terminal: -

```
+ J:\ES6FeatureDemo>node dist/default_value/example1.js
x Result:  5

  J:\ES6FeatureDemo>
```

Example: Default parameter with Object

The **src/default_value/example2.js** file contains the code to instantiate object with default values assigned to object properties. The code content of **src/default_value/example2.js** file are as follows: -

```javascript
//Object property with default value
var Student = function(name, score = 0, subject = "Mathematics"){
    this.name = name;
    this.score = score;
    this.subject = subject;
};
var student1 = new Student("Sandeep");
console.log("Student name: ",student1.name);
console.log("Student score: ",student1.score);
console.log("Student subject: ",student1.subject);
```

In the previous code we have a **function** named **Student** which can be used as a **class** to create student **object** using **new** keyword. The **Student** function has 3 different properties **name**, **score** and **subject**. The default values of **score** and **subject** are **0** and **Mathematics**. Now we can run the gulp **task** to generate the babelified code. The content of **dist/default_value/example2.js** file are as follows: -

```javascript
//Object property with default value
"use strict";
var Student = function Student(name) {
    var score = arguments.length <= 1 || arguments[1] === undefined ? 0 :
arguments[1];
    var subject = arguments.length <= 2 || arguments[2] === undefined ?
"Mathematics" : arguments[2];

    this.name = name;
    this.score = score;
    this.subject = subject;
};
var student1 = new Student("Sandeep");
console.log("Student name: ", student1.name);
```

```
console.log("Student score: ", student1.score);
console.log("Student subject: ", student1.subject);
```

From the previous code we can observe that Babel has compiled the code to generate the supported javascript code. Now we can run **dist/default_value/example2.js** code using **node dist/ default_value/example2.js** command. We have created a student object **student1** with **name** as **sandeep**. We have not passed the score and subject for **student1**. The default value for **score** and **subject** will be used in **student1** object. The following screenshot shows the terminal with node execution and output in terminal: -

```
Terminal                                                    ⚙- ↧

+  J:\ES6FeatureDemo>node dist/default_value/example2.js
✕  Student name:   Sandeep
   Student score:   0
   Student subject:   Mathematics

   J:\ES6FeatureDemo>▯
```

Summary

In this chapter we have learnt about default values for parameter with coded example. In the next chapter we will learn more ES6 features. Till then stay tuned.

Classes and Inheritance

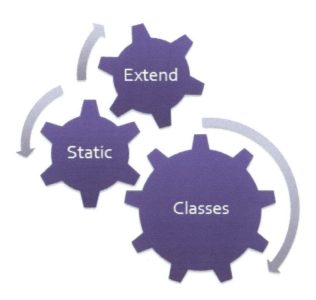

In the previous chapter we have learnt about initializing parameters with default value in this chapter we will learn about classes and inheritance. ES6 classes provides following features to object oriented programming(**OOP**): -

- **Constructors**: A class is a special type of subroutine called to create an object. It prepares the new object for use, often accepting arguments that the constructor uses to set required member variables.
- **Inheritance**: It can be defined as the process where one class acquires the properties (methods and fields) of another class.
- **Super calls**: The super keyword is a reference variable that is used to refer immediate parent class object.
- **Static methods**: Static properties are member methods and fields of a class and can be called without creating a object.

Implementing Class

ES6 provides a syntactic sugar over prototype based class declaration using **class** keyword. The updated project **ES6FeatureDemo** structure look like following screenshot: -

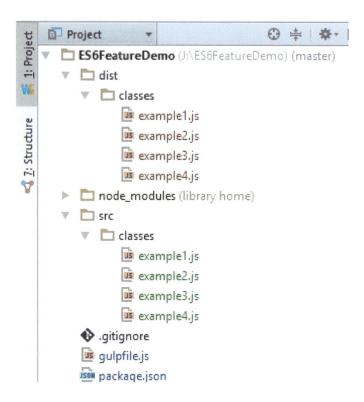

We have created a **classes** directory inside **src** folder to demonstrate ES6 classes and inheritance. The compiled code produced by Gulp task is present in **dist** folder in respective example files. Now we can develop some example to demonstrate default values of parameters.

Example: Class Declaration

The **src/classes/example1.js** file contains the code for defining a **class** and a **constructor**. The code content of **src/classes/example1.js** file are as follows: -

```
//Class declaration
class Student {
    constructor(name, subject, score) {
        this.name = name;
        this.subject = subject;
        this.score = score;
    }
}
var student1 = new Student("Sandeep","Geography",20);
var student2 = new Student("Jack","History",45);
console.log("student1: ",student1);
console.log("student2: ",student2);
```

In the previous code we have declared a class named **Student** with a parameterized constructor function. The constructor function takes 3 input parameters **name**, **subject** and **score** and assigns it to an object instance using **this** keyword. We have created 2 student object **student1** and **student2** using **new** keyword and **Student** class. Finally, we are logging both **student1** and **student2** object in the console. Now we can run the **gulp** task to generate the babelified code. The code content of **dist/classes/example1.js** file are as follows: -

```javascript
"use strict";
function _classCallCheck(instance, Constructor) { if (!(instance instanceof Constructor)) { throw new TypeError("Cannot call a class as a function"); } }
//Class declaration
var Student = function Student(name, subject, score) {
  _classCallCheck(this, Student);
  this.name = name;
  this.subject = subject;
  this.score = score;
};
var student1 = new Student("Sandeep", "Geography", 20);
var student2 = new Student("Jack", "History", 45);
console.log("student1: ", student1);
console.log("student2: ", student2);
```

From the previous code we can observe that Babel has compiled the code to generate the supported javascript code. Now we can run **dist/classes/example1.js** code using **node dist/classes/example1.js** command. The following screenshot shows the terminal with node execution and output in terminal: -

```
Terminal                                                          ⚙· ⊥
+  J:\ES6FeatureDemo>node dist/classes/example1.js
✗  student1:  Student { name: 'Sandeep', subject: 'Geography', score: 20 }
   student2:  Student { name: 'Jack', subject: 'History', score: 45 }

   J:\ES6FeatureDemo>█
```

Example: Methods in Class

The **src/classes/example2.js** file contains the code for defining **method** in a class. The code content of **src/classes/example2.js** file are as follows: -

```javascript
//Methods in Class
class Student {
  constructor(name, subject, score) {
    this.name = name;
    this.subject = subject;
    this.score = score;
  }
  getResult(){
    return this.score > 30? "PASS" : "FAIL";
  }
}
var student1 = new Student(" Sandeep","Geography",20);
var student2 = new Student("Jack","History",45);
```

```
        console.log("student1: ",student1.getResult());
        console.log("student2: ",student2.getResult());
```

In the previous code we have defined a **Student** class with parameterized **constructor** and a method name **getResult()**. This method return the **PASS** or **FAIL** based on the score. We have created 2 student object **student1** and **student2** and called the **getResult()** method. Now we can run the **gulp** task to generate the babelified code. The code content of **dist/classes/example2.js** file are as follows: -

```javascript
"use strict";
var _createClass = (function() {
  function defineProperties(target, props) {
    for (var i = 0; i < props.length; i++) {
      var descriptor = props[i];
      descriptor.enumerable = descriptor.enumerable || false;
      descriptor.configurable = true;
      if ("value" in descriptor) descriptor.writable = true;
      Object.defineProperty(target, descriptor.key, descriptor);
    }
  }
  return function(Constructor, protoProps, staticProps) {
    if (protoProps) defineProperties(Constructor.prototype,
      protoProps);
    if (staticProps) defineProperties(Constructor, staticProps);
    return Constructor;
  };
})();

function _classCallCheck(instance, Constructor) {
  if (!(instance instanceof Constructor)) {
    throw new TypeError("Cannot call a class as a function");
  }
}
//Class declaration with methods
var Student = (function() {
  function Student(name, subject, score) {
    _classCallCheck(this, Student);
    this.name = name;
    this.subject = subject;
    this.score = score;
  }
  _createClass(Student, [{
    key: "getResult",
    value: function getResult() {
      return this.score > 30 ? "PASS" : "FAIL";
    }
  }]);
  return Student;
})();
```

```javascript
var student1 = new Student("Sandeep", "Geography", 20);
var student2 = new Student("Jack", "History", 45);
console.log("student1: ", student1.getResult());
console.log("student2: ", student2.getResult());
```

From the previous code we can observe that Babel has compiled the code to generate the supported javascript code. Now we can run **dist/classes/example1.js** code using **node dist/classes/example1.js** command. The following screenshot shows the terminal with node execution and output in terminal: -

```
Terminal                                                    ⚙ ⬇

+  J:\ES6FeatureDemo>node dist/classes/example2.js
✕  student1:   FAIL
   student2:   PASS

   J:\ES6FeatureDemo>█
```

Example: Inheritance Using Extend and Super

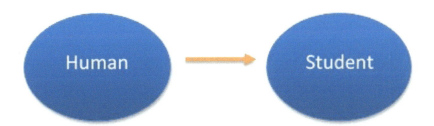

The **src/classes/example3.js** file contains the code for demonstrating **super** and **extend** keyword. The code content of **src/classes/example3.js** file are as follows: -

```javascript
//Inheritance Class Using extend and super
//parent class
class Human{
    constructor(name, country) {
        this.name = name;
        this.country = country;
    }
}
//Child class
class Student extends Human{
    constructor(name, country, subject, score) {
        super(name, country);
        this.subject = subject;
        this.score = score;
    }
```

```
        getResult(){
            return this.score > 30? "PASS" : "FAIL";
        }
    }
    var student1 = new Student("Sandeep","India","Geography",20);
    var student2 = new Student("Jack", "South Africa","History",45);
    console.log("student1: ",student1.getResult());
    console.log("student2: ",student2.getResult());
```

In the previous code we have created 2 class **Human** and **Student**. The **Human** class has 2 property **name** and **country** in its **constructor** function. The **Student** class is the **derived** from **Human** class using **extend** keyword. The **Student** class constructor takes 4 parameters **name**, **country**, **subject** and **score**. The **Student** class constructor calls and initializes the **Human** constructor by passing **name** and **country** parameter using **super()** function. We have created **student1** and **student2** object and logged the result returned by **getResult()** method. Now we can run the **gulp** task to generate the babelified code. The code content of **dist/classes/example3.js** file are as follows: -

```
    "use strict";
    var _createClass = (function() {
        function defineProperties(target, props) {
            for (var i = 0; i < props.length; i++) {
                var descriptor = props[i];
                descriptor.enumerable = descriptor.enumerable || false;
                descriptor.configurable = true;
                if ("value" in descriptor) descriptor.writable = true;
                Object.defineProperty(target, descriptor.key, descriptor);
            }
        }
        return function(Constructor, protoProps, staticProps) {
            if (protoProps) defineProperties(Constructor.prototype,
                protoProps);
            if (staticProps) defineProperties(Constructor, staticProps);
            return Constructor;
        };
    })();

    function _possibleConstructorReturn(self, call) {
        if (!self) {
            throw new ReferenceError(
                "this hasn't been initialised - super() hasn't been called");
        }
        return call && (typeof call === "object" || typeof call ===
        "function") ? call : self;
    }

    function _inherits(subClass, superClass) {
        if (typeof superClass !== "function" && superClass !== null) {
```

```javascript
      throw new TypeError(
        "Super expression must either be null or a function, not " +
        typeof superClass);
    }
    subClass.prototype = Object.create(superClass && superClass.prototype, {
      constructor: {
        value: subClass,
        enumerable: false,
        writable: true,
        configurable: true
      }
    });
    if (superClass) Object.setPrototypeOf ? Object.setPrototypeOf(
      subClass, superClass) : subClass.__proto__ = superClass;
}

function _classCallCheck(instance, Constructor) {
  if (!(instance instanceof Constructor)) {
    throw new TypeError("Cannot call a class as a function");
  }
}

//Inheritance Class Using extend and super
var Human = function Human(name, country) {
  _classCallCheck(this, Human);
  this.name = name;
  this.country = country;
};

var Student = (function(_Human) {
  _inherits(Student, _Human);
  function Student(name, country, subject, score) {
    _classCallCheck(this, Student);
    var _this = _possibleConstructorReturn(this, Object.getPrototypeOf(
      Student).call(this, name, country));
    _this.subject = subject;
    _this.score = score;
    return _this;
  }
  _createClass(Student, [{
    key: "getResult",
    value: function getResult() {
      return this.score > 30 ? "PASS" : "FAIL";
    }
  }]);
  return Student;
})(Human);

var student1 = new Student("Sandeep", "India", "Geography", 20);
```

```
var student2 = new Student("Jack", "South Africa", "History", 45);
console.log("student1: ", student1.getResult());
console.log("student2: ", student2.getResult());
```

From the previous code we can observe that Babel has compiled the code to generate the supported javascript code. Now we can run **dist/classes/example3.js** code using **node dist/classes/example3.js** command. The following screenshot shows the terminal with node execution and output in terminal: -

```
Terminal                                              ⚙ ⬇
+  J:\ES6FeatureDemo>node dist/classes/example3.js
✗  student1:   FAIL
   student2:   PASS

   J:\ES6FeatureDemo>|
```

Example: Defining Static Method

The **src/classes/example4.js** file contains the code for defining **static** properties in a class. To define a static member, **static** keyword is **prefixed** before the properties. The code content of **src/classes/example4.js** file are as follows: -

```
//static method in class
class Util{
    static getSquare(number){
        return number * number;
    }
};
var result = Util.getSquare(5);
console.log("Result: ",result);
```

In the previous code we have created Util class. The **Util** class has static member function named **getSquare().** This method takes a number as input parameter and **returns** the **square.** As **getSquare()** method is static in nature we can directly call it through **Util** class without creating any instance of it. Now we can run the **gulp** task to generate the babelified code. The code content of **dist/classes/example4.js** file are as follows: -

```
"use strict";
var _createClass = (function() {
    function defineProperties(target, props) {
        for (var i = 0; i < props.length; i++) {
            var descriptor = props[i];
            descriptor.enumerable = descriptor.enumerable || false;
            descriptor.configurable = true;
            if ("value" in descriptor) descriptor.writable = true;
            Object.defineProperty(target, descriptor.key, descriptor);
```

```javascript
        }
      }
      return function(Constructor, protoProps, staticProps) {
        if (protoProps) defineProperties(Constructor.prototype,
          protoProps);
        if (staticProps) defineProperties(Constructor, staticProps);
        return Constructor;
      };
    })();

    function _classCallCheck(instance, Constructor) {
      if (!(instance instanceof Constructor)) {
        throw new TypeError("Cannot call a class as a function");
      }
    }

    var Util = (function() {
      function Util() {
        _classCallCheck(this, Util);
      }
      _createClass(Util, null, [{
        key: "getSquare",
        value: function getSquare(number) {
          return number * number;
        }
      }]);
      return Util;
    })();
    var result = Util.getSquare(5);
    console.log("Result: ", result);
```

From the previous code we can observe that Babel has compiled the code to generate the supported javascript code. Now we can run **dist/classes/example4.js** code using **node dist/classes/example4.js** command. The following screenshot shows the terminal with node execution and output in terminal: -

```
Terminal                                              ⚙ ▾  ⤓
 + J:\ES6FeatureDemo>node dist/classes/example4.js
 ✕ Result:    25

   J:\ES6FeatureDemo>
```

Summary

In this chapter we have learnt about default values for parameter with coded example. In the next chapter we will learn more ES6 features. Till then stay tuned.

7

Object Initializer and Property

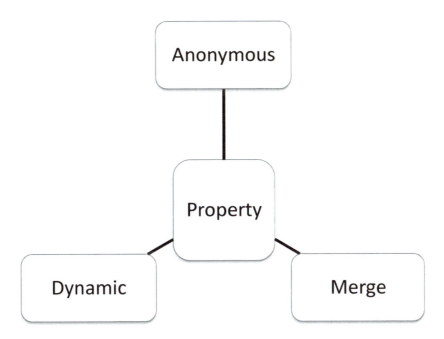

In the previous chapter we have learnt about classes. in this chapter we will learn about object properties. An object literal initializer is a list of zero or more pairs of property names and associated values of an object, enclosed in curly braces. Objects consist of properties, which are used to describe an object. Object literals looks like a JSON object but has many features compared to JSON. The key differences between object literals and JSON object are as follows: -

- JSON permits only properties declaration using key-value pair. In object literals we can defines methods too.
- In JSON object a value can be a strings, numbers, arrays, true, false, null, or another JSON object. In object literal we can also have function as value.

Implementing Class

ES6 provides Object literal notation to create Object. The updated project **ES6FeatureDemo** structure look like following screenshot: -

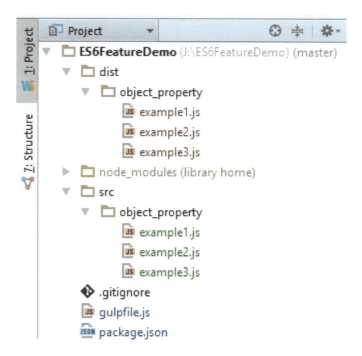

We have created an **object property** directory inside **src** folder to demonstrate Object literal initializer. The compiled code produced by Gulp task is present in **dist** folder in respective example files. Now we can develop some example to demonstrate object literal to define properties.

Example: Merging Object Properties

The **src/object_property/example1.js** file contains the code for defining a **class** and a **constructor**. The code content of **src/object_property/example1.js** file are as follows: -

```
//Merging object properties using assign method
let aStudent = { name:"sandeep", country:"india"};
let aStatus = {subject:"Geography" ,score:30};
console.log("aStudent Before assign: ",aStudent);
Object.assign(aStudent,aStatus);
console.log("aStudent After assign: ",aStudent);
```

In the previous code we have declared 2 objects named **aStudent** and **aStatus**. The **aStudent** object contains 2 property **name** and **country**. The **aStatus** object contains 2 property **subject** and **score**. The **Object.assign()** method is used to **merge** the properties of **aStatus** to **aStudent**. Now we can run the **gulp** task to generate the babelified code. The code content of **dist/object_property/example1.js** file are as follows: -

```
"use strict";
//Merging object properties using assign method
```

```
var aStudent = { name: "sandeep", country: "india" };
var aStatus = { subject: "Geography", score: 30 };
console.log("aStudent Before assign: ", aStudent);
Object.assign(aStudent, aStatus);
console.log("aStudent After assign: ", aStudent);
```

From the previous code we can observe that Babel has compiled the code to generate the supported javascript code. As we are using latest NodeJS library and it support **Object.assign()** method, the babelified code is same. Now we can run **dist/object_property/example1.js** code using **node dist/object_property/example1.js** command. The following screenshot shows the terminal with node execution and output in terminal: -

```
Terminal                                              ⚙ ⬇

+  J:\ES6FeatureDemo>node dist/object_property/example1.js
✕  aStudent Before assign:  { name: 'sandeep', country: 'india' }
   aStudent After assign:  { name: 'sandeep',
     country: 'india',
     subject: 'Geography',
     score: 30 }

   J:\ES6FeatureDemo>▮
```

Example: Object initialization using Shorthand

The **src/object_property/example2.js** file contains the code for demonstrating shorthand approach to define an object. The code content of **src/object_property/example2.js** file are as follows: -

```
//Object initialization using Shorthand
let name='sandeep';
let subject = "Geography";
let aStudent = {name, subject};
console.log("aStudent: ", aStudent);
```

In the previous code we have defined two variable **name** and **subject** containing values **sandeep** and **Geography**. Now we can run the **gulp** task to generate the babelified code. The code content of **dist/object_property/example2.js** file are as follows: -

```
"use strict";
//Object initialization using Shorthand
var name = 'sandeep';
var subject = "Geography";
var aStudent = { name: name, subject: subject };
console.log("aStudent: ", aStudent);
```

From the previous code we can observe that Babel has compiled the code to generate the supported javascript code. Now we can run **dist/object_property/example2.js** code using **node dist/object_property/example2.js** command. The following screenshot shows the terminal with node execution and output in terminal: -

```
Terminal                                                              ⚙ ▾  ⤓
+  J:\ES6FeatureDemo>node dist/object_property/example2.js
×  aStudent:  { name: 'sandeep', subject: 'Geography' }

   J:\ES6FeatureDemo>█
```

Example: Dynamic Property

The **src/object_property/example3.js** file contains the code for demonstrating dynamic property initialization for an object. The code content of **src/object_property/example3.js** file are as follows: -

```javascript
//Dynamic property
var property1='name';
var property2='subject';
var aStudent = {
    [property1]:"Sandeep",
    [property2]:"Computer Science"
};
console.log("aStudent: ",aStudent);
```

In the previous code we have 2 variables **property1** and **property2** having string content **name** and **subject**. The **aStudent** variable is defined as an anonymous object. The **aStudent** object has 2 fields **property1** and **property2** surrounded by **square bracket []**. A property in an object is a **key-value** pair separated by semicolon. In this case **[property1]** and **[property2]** are the keys where **sandeep** and **computer science** are values. The following diagram shows the pictorial relationship between key and value combination to make a complete property.

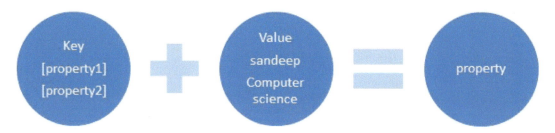

The **square bracket** is used for defining dynamic property. During runtime the **[property1]** and **[property2]** will take the corresponding value **name** and **subject** from the variables dynamically and result in an object **aStudent**. Now **aStudent** object has 2 property **name** and **subject**. Now we can run the **gulp** task to generate the babelified code. The code content of **dist/object_property/example3.js** file are as follows: -

```javascript
'use strict';
var _aStudent;
function _defineProperty(obj, key, value) {
  if (key in obj) {
    Object.defineProperty(obj, key, {
      value: value,
      enumerable: true,
      configurable: true,
      writable: true
    });
  } else {
    obj[key] = value;
  }
  return obj;
}
//Dynamic property
var property1 = 'name';
var property2 = 'subject';
var aStudent = (_aStudent = {}, _defineProperty(_aStudent, property1,
  "Sandeep"), _defineProperty(_aStudent, property2,
  "Computer Science"), _aStudent);
console.log("aStudent: ", aStudent);
```

From the previous code we can observe that Babel has compiled the code to generate the supported javascript code. Now we can run **dist/object_property/example3.js** code using **node dist/object_property/example3.js** command. The following screenshot shows the terminal with node execution and output in terminal: -

```
Terminal                                                    ⚙ ▾  ⬲
+  J:\ES6FeatureDemo>node dist/object_property/example3.js
✗  aStudent:  { name: 'Sandeep', subject: 'Computer Science' }

   J:\ES6FeatureDemo>█
```

Summary

In this chapter we have learnt Object initializer with coded example. In the next chapter we will learn more ES6 features. Till then stay tuned.

8

Template String

In the previous chapter we have learnt about Object properties. in this chapter we will learn about template string. If you are a javascript developer, then you might have known how a templating library can help the developer to reduce effort by reducing line of code to do. There are many libraries like Handlebar, dust.js exists to implement templating system in project.ES6 brings similar templating mechanism that can be used natively by a javascript developer. Some of the important features of ES6 templating string are as follows: -

- **Expression placeholder**, it enables a developer to used javascript expression inside a template string which can be executed during run time.
- **Function Expression**, it enables a developer to call a javascript inbuilt or custom function inside a templating string.
- **Tagging Function**, it enables a developer to tag any javascript function that can be used with a templating string. the literals and substitutions are passed to the tag function, and whatever returns from the function is the resulting value.

A **template string** is represented by surrounding **back-ticks (``)**. A **template placeholder** expression is represented with dollar and 2 curly braced **${}**. The syntax for template string and placeholder expression are as follows: -

```
`a string`
${placeholder}
```

Implementing Template String

ES6 provides template string to implement templating mechanism. The updated project **ES6FeatureDemo** structure look like following screenshot: -

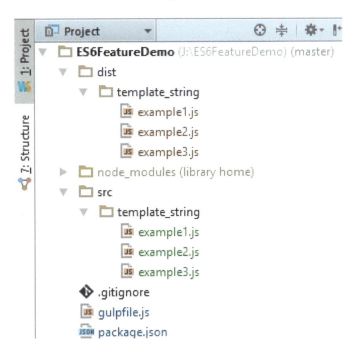

We have created a **template_string** directory inside **src** folder to demonstrate ES6 template string feature. The compiled code produced by Gulp task is present in **dist** folder in respective example files. Now we can develop some example to demonstrate template string.

Example: Value Substitution

The **src/template_string/example1.js** file contains the code for defining a template placeholder. The code content of **src/template_string/example1.js** file are as follows: -

```
//Value substitution
var aStudent = {
    name:"Sandeep Kumar Patel",
    subject:"Computer"
};
var studentDetail = `Name: ${aStudent.name}\nSubject: ${aStudent.subject}`;
console.log(studentDetail);
```

In the previous code we have declared an object named **aStudent**. The **aStudent** object contains 2 property **name** and **subject**. We have declared **studentDetail** variable which contains a template string surrounded by **back-ticks**. The template string has 2 placeholder named **${aStudentName}** and **${aStudent.subject}**. These template placeholders will take the value for **aStudent** object. Now we can run the **gulp** task to generate the babelified code. The code content of **dist/template_string/example1.js** file are as follows: -

```
"use strict";
//Value substitution
var aStudent = {
    name: "Sandeep Kumar Patel",
    subject: "Computer"
};
var studentDetail = "Name: " + aStudent.name + "\nSubject: " + aStudent.subject;
console.log(studentDetail);
```

From the previous code we can observe that Babel has compiled the code to generate the supported javascript code. Now we can run **dist/template_string/example1.js** code using **node dist/template_string/example1.js** command. The following screenshot shows the terminal with node execution and output in terminal: -

```
Terminal                                          ✿ ⋅  ↓
+  J:\ES6FeatureDemo>node dist/template_string/example1.js
✕  Name: Sandeep Kumar Patel
   Subject: Computer


   J:\ES6FeatureDemo>
```

Example: Function in template string

The **src/template_string/example2.js** file contains the code for defining a template placeholder. The code content of **src/template_string/example2.js** file are as follows: -

```
//Function in template string
var getResult = function(score){
    return score > 30 ? "PASS":"FAIL";
};
var message = `Student ${getResult(60)} with score 60`;
console.log(message);
```

In the previous code we have declared a method named **getResult()**. This method takes score as input parameter and returns **PASS** or **FAIL** status. If the **score** is **less** than **30**, It return **FAIL** and **greater** then **30**, it returns **PASS**. There a template string variable named **message**. This template string has a place holder **${getResult(60)}** which calls the **getResult()** method with input score **60**. Now we can run the **gulp** task to generate the babelified code. The code content of **dist/template_string/example2.js** file are as follows: -

```
"use strict";
//Function in template string
var getResult = function getResult(score) {
    return score > 30 ? "PASS" : "FAIL";
};
var message = "Student " + getResult(60) + " with score 60";
console.log(message);
```

From the previous code we can observe that Babel has compiled the code to generate the supported javascript code. Now we can run **dist/template_string/example2.js** code using **node dist/template_string/example2.js** command. The following screenshot shows the terminal with node execution and output in terminal: -

```
Terminal                                              ⚙▾  ⬇

+  J:\ES6FeatureDemo>node dist/template_string/example2.js
✕  Student PASS with score 60


   J:\ES6FeatureDemo>█
```

Example: Tagged template string

The **src/template_string/example3.js** file contains the code for defining a template placeholder. The code content of **src/template_string/example3.js** file are as follows: -

```javascript
//Tagged template String
var sayHello = function(input){
    return "Hello "+input;
};
var result1 = sayHello `Sandeep`;
console.log("Result1: "+result1);

var doSquare = function(number){
    return number * number;
};
let aNumber = 5;
var result2 = doSquare `5`;
console.log("Result2: "+result2);
```

In the previous code we have declared 2 methods **sayHello()** and **doSquare()**. The **sayHello()** method takes a string and returns a string **prefixed** with **Hello**. The **doSquare()** method takes a **number** as input and returns the **square** of it. Both of these methods are used as a tag and can be used with a template string. Now we can run the **gulp** task to generate the babelified code. The code content of **dist/template_string/example3.js** file are as follows: -

```javascript
"use strict";
var _templateObject = _taggedTemplateLiteral(["Sandeep"], ["Sandeep"]),
    _templateObject2 = _taggedTemplateLiteral(["5"], ["5"]);

function _taggedTemplateLiteral(strings, raw) {
    return Object.freeze(Object.defineProperties(strings, {
        raw: {
            value: Object.freeze(raw)
        }
    }
```

```
        }));
    }
    //Tagged template String
    var sayHello = function sayHello(input) {
        return "Hello " + input;
    };
    var result1 = sayHello(_templateObject);
    console.log("Result1: " + result1);
    var doSquare = function doSquare(number) {
        return number * number;
    };
    var aNumber = 5;
    var result2 = doSquare(_templateObject2);
    console.log("Result2: " + result2);
```

From the previous code we can observe that Babel has compiled the code to generate the supported javascript code. Now we can run **dist/template_string/example3.js** code using **node dist/template_string/example3.js** command. The following screenshot shows the terminal with node execution and output in terminal: -

```
Terminal                                                    ⚙ ⏬
+  J:\ES6FeatureDemo>node dist/template_string/example3.js
✗  Result1: Hello Sandeep
   Result2: 25


   J:\ES6FeatureDemo>▊
```

Summary

In this chapter we have learnt about template string with coded example. We have also tested a tag function for template string. In the next chapter we will learn more ES6 features. Till then stay tuned.

9

Promise Object

In the previous chapter we have learnt about template string. in this chapter we will learn about Promise object. A promise object represents an object whose value is not known now but will be known sometime in near future. A promise is a commitment made, an agreement or assurance, an oath taken for something by someone.

Promise object support deferred and asynchronous execution of JavaScript. and helps in resolving Blocking nature of JavaScript. A promise object can have one of the 3 states listed as follows: -

- **pending**: It represents the initial state of the promise object which is not yet resolved or rejected.
- **fulfilled**: It represents the resolved state of a promise object and all the operation mentioned for the promise object has been executed successfully.
- **rejected**: It represents the failed states of a promise object and the operations mentioned in promise object has not been executed completely.

A promise object is cared using new keyword and promise constructor which takes an executor function with resolve and reject object. The syntax for defining a promise object is as follows: -

```
new Promise(function(resolve, reject) {
  //...
});
```

Implementing Promise Object

ES6 provides promise object to work with Asynchronous code which provides deferred execution environment. The updated project **ES6FeatureDemo** structure look like following screenshot: -

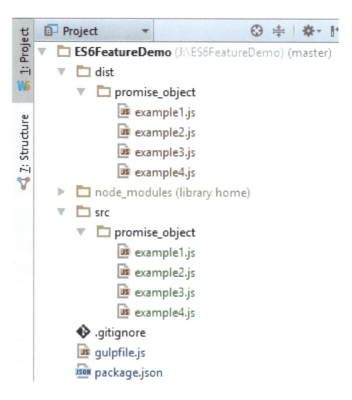

We have created a **promise_object** directory inside **src** folder to demonstrate ES6 promise feature. The compiled code produced by Gulp task is present in **dist** folder in respective example files. Now we can develop some example to demonstrate promise.

Example: Resolving a promise

The **src/promise_object/example1.js** file contains the code for defining a simple promise object. The code content of **src/promise_object/example1.js** file are as follows: -

```javascript
//Resolving a promise
var squareOfNumber = function(number) {
  var myPromise = new Promise(function(resolve, reject) {
      resolve(number * number);
  });
  return myPromise;
};
var squarePromise1 = squareOfNumber(5);
squarePromise1.then(function(result) {
```

```
    console.log(result);
  });
```

In the previous code we have declared a method named **squareOfNumber()** . This method takes a number as input parameter and returns a **promise** object. We have used **then()** function to process the result when the promise object is resolved. Now we can run the **gulp** task to generate the babelified code. The code content of **dist/promise_object/example1.js** file are as follows: -

```
"use strict";
//Resolving a promise
var squareOfNumber = function squareOfNumber(number) {
  var myPromise = new Promise(function (resolve, reject) {
    resolve(number * number);
  });
  return myPromise;
};
var squarePromise1 = squareOfNumber(5);
squarePromise1.then(function (result) {
  console.log(result);
});
```

From the previous code we can observe that Babel has compiled the code to generate the supported javascript code. Now we can run **dist/promise_object/example1.js** code using **node dist/promise_object/example1.js** command. The following screenshot shows the terminal with node execution and output in terminal: -

```
Terminal                                              ⚙ ⌄ ⌄

+ J:\ES6FeatureDemo>node dist/promise_object/example1.js
✕ 25

  J:\ES6FeatureDemo>▮
```

Example: Rejecting a promise

The **src/promise_object/example2.js** file contains the code for defining a simple promise object with reject method. The code content of **src/promise_object/example2.js** file are as follows: -

```
//Rejecting a promise
var squareOfNumber = function(number) {
  var myPromise = new Promise(function(resolve, reject) {
    if (number > 0) {
      resolve(number * number);
    } else {
```

```
            reject(new Error("Error:It is not a positive number."));
        }
    });
    return myPromise;
};
//Passing a negative number
var squarePromise2 = squareOfNumber(-4);
squarePromise2.then(null, function(error) {
    console.log(error.toString());
});
```

In the previous code we have declared a method named **squareOfNumber()** . This method takes a positive number as input parameter and returns a **promise** object. We have used **then()** function to process the result when the promise object is resolved. If we pass a negative number, then it will be rejected using reject method with an error object. Now we can run the **gulp** task to generate the babelified code. The code content of **dist/promise_object/example2.js** file are as follows: -

```
"use strict";
//Rejecting a promise
var squareOfNumber = function squareOfNumber(number) {
    var myPromise = new Promise(function (resolve, reject) {
        if (number > 0) {
            resolve(number * number);
        } else {
            reject(new Error("Error:It is not a positive number."));
        }
    });
    return myPromise;
};
//Passing a negative number
var squarePromise2 = squareOfNumber(-4);
squarePromise2.then(null, function (error) {
    console.log(error.toString());
});
```

From the previous code we can observe that Babel has compiled the code to generate the supported javascript code. Now we can run **dist/promise_object/example2.js** code using **node dist/promise_object/example2.js** command. The following screenshot shows the terminal with node execution and output in terminal: -

Example: Multiple promise object

The **src/promise_object/example3.js** file contains the code for defining multiple objects.

The code content of **src/promise_object/example3.js** file are as follows: -

```javascript
//Multiple promises
//Returns student object array
var getAllStudent = function(){
    var studentPromise = new Promise(function(resolve, reject) {
        resolve([
            {"roll":3, "name":"John"},
            {"roll":2, "name":"Sandeep"},
            {"roll":1, "name":"Smith"}
        ]);
    });
    return studentPromise;
};
//Returns score object array
var getAllScore = function(){
    var scorePromise = new Promise(function(resolve, reject) {
        resolve([
            {"roll":2, "score":43},
            {"roll":3, "score":35},
            {"roll":1, "score":65}
        ]);
    });
    return scorePromise;
};

var studentPromise = getAllStudent();
var scorePromise = getAllScore();
Promise.all([studentPromise, scorePromise]).then(function (values) {
    var students = values[0];
    var scores = values[1];
    for(let aStudent of students){
        var targetScore = scores.find(aScore=> aScore.roll === aStudent.roll);
        console.log(aStudent.name+" with roll "+aStudent.roll+" has score
"+targetScore.score);
    }
});
```

In the previous code we have declared a 2 methods **getAllStudent()** and **getAllScore()**. Bothe of these method returns a promise object referred by variable **studentPromise** and **scorePromise**. The **all()** method is used for handling promise object and when all the input promise objects are resolved or rejected then the callback function will be executed. The callback function has **for...of** method to iterate students array and for each iteration a scores array is used with **find()** method with predicates for given roll number and displayed the details of student. Now we can run the **gulp** task to generate the babelified code. The code content of **dist/promise_object/example3.js** file are as follows: -

```javascript
"use strict";
//Multiple promises
//Returns student object array
var getAllStudent = function getAllStudent() {
  var studentPromise = new Promise(function (resolve, reject) {
    resolve([{ "roll": 3, "name": "John" }, { "roll": 2, "name": "Sandeep" }, { "roll":
1, "name": "Smith" }]);
  });
  return studentPromise;
};
//Returns score object array
var getAllScore = function getAllScore() {
  var scorePromise = new Promise(function (resolve, reject) {
    resolve([{ "roll": 2, "score": 43 }, { "roll": 3, "score": 35 }, { "roll": 1, "score":
65 }]);
  });
  return scorePromise;
};

var studentPromise = getAllStudent();
var scorePromise = getAllScore();
Promise.all([studentPromise, scorePromise]).then(function (values) {
  var students = values[0];
  var scores = values[1];
  var _iteratorNormalCompletion = true;
  var _didIteratorError = false;
  var _iteratorError = undefined;

  try {
    var _loop = function _loop() {
      var aStudent = _step.value;
      targetScore = scores.find(function (aScore) {
        return aScore.roll === aStudent.roll;
      });

      console.log(aStudent.name + " with roll " + aStudent.roll + " has score " +
targetScore.score);
    };
```

```
        for (var _iterator = students[Symbol.iterator](), _step;
    !(_iteratorNormalCompletion = (_step = _iterator.next()).done);
    _iteratorNormalCompletion = true) {
            var targetScore;

            _loop();
        }
    } catch (err) {
        _didIteratorError = true;
        _iteratorError = err;
    } finally {
        try {
            if (!_iteratorNormalCompletion && _iterator.return) {
                _iterator.return();
            }
        } finally {
            if (_didIteratorError) {
                throw _iteratorError;
            }
        }
    }
});
```

From the previous code we can observe that Babel has compiled the code to generate the supported javascript code. Now we can run **dist/promise_object/example3.js** code using **node dist/promise_object/example3.js** command. The following screenshot shows the terminal with node execution and output in terminal: -

```
Terminal                                                    ⚙ ⤓
+  J:\ES6FeatureDemo>node dist/promise_object/example3.js
✕  John with roll 3 has score 35
   Sandeep with roll 2 has score 43
   Smith with roll 1 has score 65


   J:\ES6FeatureDemo>▮
```

Example: Race Condition

The **src/promise_object/example4.js** file contains the code for defining a simple promise object. The code content of **src/promise_object/example4.js** file are as follows: -

```
//Race condition with Promise
var promise1 = new Promise(function(resolve, reject){
    setTimeout(function(){
        resolve("promise1 resolved after 500 milli seconds")
    },500);
```

```
});
var promise2 = new Promise(function(resolve, reject){
   setTimeout(function(){
       resolve("promise2 resolved after 100 milli seconds")
   },100);
});

Promise.race([promise1, promise2]).then(function (values) {
   var fromPromise = values;
   console.log("fromPromise ",fromPromise);
});
```

In the previous code we have declared 2 promise **promise1** and **promised2** objects. The **race()** method is used for handling multiple promises. Unlike **all()** method race method does not wait for all the promises. Any of the input promise is resolved/rejected the callback function will be executed. For this example the **promise2** is resolved earlier as it has 100 milli seconds to wait for and the callback function of **race()** method will have the only value from **promise2**.Now we can run the **gulp** task to generate the babelified code. The code content of **dist/promise_object/example4.js** file are as follows: -

```
"use strict";
//Race condition with Promise
var promise1 = new Promise(function (resolve, reject) {
   setTimeout(function () {
       resolve("promise1 resolved after 500 milli seconds");
   }, 500);
});
var promise2 = new Promise(function (resolve, reject) {
   setTimeout(function () {
       resolve("promise2 resolved after 100 milli seconds");
   }, 100);
});

Promise.race([promise1, promise2]).then(function (values) {
   var fromPromise = values;
   console.log("fromPromise ", fromPromise);
});
```

From the previous code we can observe that Babel has compiled the code to generate the supported javascript code. Now we can run **dist/promise_object/example4.js** code using **node dist/promise_object/example4.js** command. The following screenshot shows the terminal with node execution and output in terminal: -

```
Terminal                                              ⚙ ⏚
+  J:\ES6FeatureDemo>node dist/promise_object/example4.js
✕  fromPromise  promise2 resolved after 100 milli seconds

   J:\ES6FeatureDemo>█
```

Summary

In this chapter we have learnt about defining a promise object. We have also explored the methods resolve and reject with coded example. In the next chapter we will learn more ES6 features. Till then stay tuned.

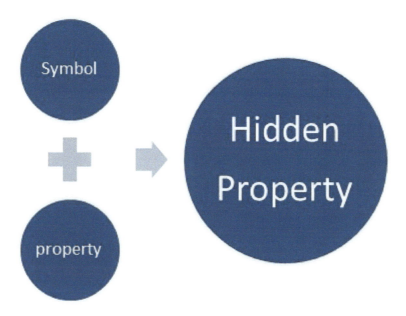

In the previous chapter we have learnt about Promise object. in this chapter we will learn about Symbols. To make a property almost private, you could use the new Symbol data type to generate a property name and store it in a Module together with the class. symbols are unique and immutable. their only use is to avoid name clashes between properties. Some of the important points for Symbols are as follows: -

- Symbols can be created as local or in global scope as a shared symbol. The symbols created in global scope has to register in **Global symbol registry**.
- The properties defined using symbols are not visible to **for...in** loop and cannot be listed in **getOwnPropertyNames()** method.

Implementing Symbols

ES6 provides Symbol to create hidden properties. The updated project **ES6FeatureDemo** structure look like following screenshot: -

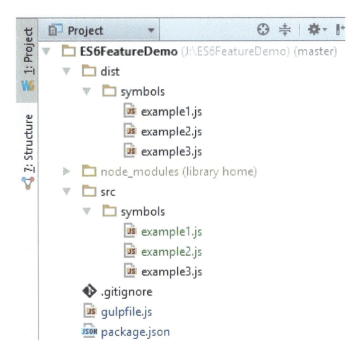

We have created a **symbols** directory inside **src** folder to demonstrate ES6 promise feature. The compiled code produced by Gulp task is present in **dist** folder in respective example files. Now we can develop some example to demonstrate symbols.

Example: Primitive local symbol type

The **src/symbols/example1.js** file contains the code for defining a primitive symbol type. The code content of **src/symbols/example1.js** file are as follows: -

```
//Primitive local symbol type
var  symbol1 = Symbol("I am Symbol1");
console.log("symbol1: ",symbol1);
var symbol1Type = typeof symbol1;
console.log("symbol1Type: ",symbol1Type);
```

In the previous code we have declared a symbol named **symbol1** and then checked the type of **symbol1** using **typeof** operator. Now we can run the **gulp** task to generate the babelified code. The code content of **dist/symbols/example1.js** file are as follows: -

```
"use strict";
function _typeof(obj) {
    return obj && obj.constructor === Symbol ? "symbol" : typeof obj;
}
//Primitive local symbol type
var symbol1 = Symbol("I am Symbol1");
console.log("symbol1: ", symbol1);
var symbol1Type = typeof symbol1 === "undefined" ? "undefined" :
    _typeof(symbol1);
console.log("symbol1Type: ", symbol1Type);
```

From the previous code we can observe that Babel has compiled the code to generate the supported javascript code. Now we can run **dist/symbols/example1.js** code using **node dist/symbols/example1.js** command. The following screenshot shows the terminal with node execution and output in terminal: -

```
Terminal                                                          ⚙ ⏬
+  J:\ES6FeatureDemo>node dist/symbols/example1.js
✕  symbol1:  Symbol(I am Symbol1)
   symbol1Type:  symbol

   J:\ES6FeatureDemo>█
```

Example: Searching global symbol registry

The **src/symbols/example2.js** file contains the code for defining a Global primitive symbol type. The code content of **src/symbols/example2.js** file are as follows: -

```javascript
//Searching Global Symbol registry
var  symbol2 = Symbol.for(24);
console.log("Key for symbol2: ",Symbol.keyFor(symbol2));
console.log("Symbol for key 24: ",Symbol.for(24));
```

In the previous code we have declared a symbol named **symbol2** using **for()** method. The **symbol2** is registered as Global shared symbol.

- The **Symbol.for()** method searches for existing symbols with the given key and returns it if found. Otherwise a new symbol gets created in the global symbol registry with this key.
- The **Symbol.keyFor()** method retrieves a shared symbol key from the global symbol registry for the given symbol.

Now we can run the **gulp** task to generate the babelified code. The code content of **dist/symbols/example2.js** file are as follows: -

```javascript
"use strict";
//Searching Global Symbol registry
var symbol2 = Symbol.for(24);
console.log("Key for symbol2: ", Symbol.keyFor(symbol2));
console.log("Symbol for key 24: ", Symbol.for(24));
```

From the previous code we can observe that Babel has compiled the code to generate the supported javascript code. Now we can run **dist/symbols/example2.js** code using **node**

dist/symbols/example2.js command. The following screenshot shows the terminal with node execution and output in terminal: -

```
Terminal                                                    ⚙ ▾  ⬇
+  J:\ES6FeatureDemo>node dist/symbols/example2.js
✕  Key for symbol2:   24
   Symbol for key 24:   Symbol(24)

   J:\ES6FeatureDemo>█
```

Example: Symbol as hidden property

The **src/symbols/example3.js** file contains the code for defining a Global primitive symbol type. The code content of **src/symbols/example3.js** file are as follows: -

```javascript
//Symbol as hidden property
var rollSymProperty = Symbol.for('roll');
var Student = function(name, roll, country, subject){
   this['name']= name;
   this[rollSymProperty] = roll;
   this['country'] = country;
   this['subject'] = subject;
};
var student1 = new Student("Sandeep", 12, "India", "Computer");
console.log("student1 Own Properties:",
Object.getOwnPropertyNames(student1));
console.log("JSON Stringify: ",JSON.stringify(student1));
console.log("student1 Own Property Symbols:
",Object.getOwnPropertySymbols(student1));
console.log("student1 has private property: ",
Symbol.keyFor(rollSymProperty)," with value: ", student1[rollSymProperty]);
```

In the previous code we have declared a **Student** function with 4 properties. The **roll** property is defined as Global symbol. We have created a Student object named **student1** and logged the list of properties for **student1**. The **JSON.stringify()** method is used to represent as JSON object. The symbol property present in **student1** is listed using **getOwnPropertySymbols()** method. Now we can run the **gulp** task to generate the babelified code. The code content of **dist/symbols/example3.js** file are as follows: -

```javascript
'use strict';
//Symbol as hidden property
```

```
var rollSymProperty = Symbol.for('roll');
var Student = function Student(name, roll, country, subject) {
    this['name'] = name;
    this[rollSymProperty] = roll;
    this['country'] = country;
    this['subject'] = subject;
};
var student1 = new Student("Sandeep", 12, "India", "Computer");

console.log("student1 Own Properties: ",
Object.getOwnPropertyNames(student1));
console.log("JSON Stringify: ", JSON.stringify(student1));

console.log("student1 Own Property Symbols: ",
Object.getOwnPropertySymbols(student1));
console.log("student1 has private property: ", Symbol.keyFor(rollSymProperty),
" with value: ", student1[rollSymProperty]);
```

From the previous code we can observe that Babel has compiled the code to generate the supported javascript code. Now we can run **dist/symbols/example3.js** code using **node dist/symbols/example3.js** command. The following screenshot shows the terminal with node execution and output in terminal: -

```
Terminal                                                          ✿ ⋅  ⊥
+  J:\ES6FeatureDemo>node dist/symbols/example3.js
✕  student1 Own Properties:  [ 'name', 'country', 'subject' ]
   JSON Stringify:  {"name":"Sandeep","country":"India","subject":"Computer"}
   student1 Own Property Symbols:  [ Symbol(roll) ]
   student1 has private property:  roll  with value:  12

   J:\ES6FeatureDemo>
```

Summary

In this chapter we have learnt about Symbols. We have also explored defining hidden property for an object with coded example. In the next chapter we will learn more ES6 features. Till then stay tuned.

11
Generators

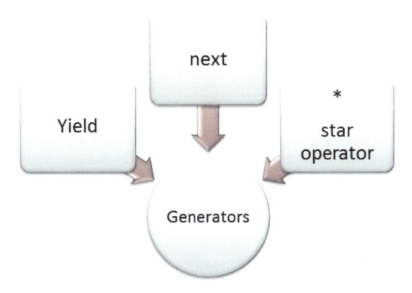

In the previous chapter we have learnt about Symbols object. in this chapter we will learn about Generators.ES6 comes with a new feature named Generator. A Generator is a special type of javascript function. The traditional javascript function has run to completion behaviour. It means once a function start executing 1st line of code it does not stop until the last statement is executed or a return statement is encountered. A generator function can be paused at any point during execution. And later can be resumed from the point where it paused last time. syntax of a ES6 generator declaration is as follows:

```
function* name([parameters]) {
    //generator definition
    yield statement;
}
```

The details of the preceding code syntax are as follows: -

- A **star * operator** is used to declare a generator function.
- A **yield** statement defines the pause point for the iterator returned by generator function. Generator function **returns** an **iterator**.
- A method **next()** can be called on this returned iterator. On call to **next()** method the Generator body gets executed up to the first yield statement.

The **yield** statement returns a value from the iterator and yield keyword returns an **IteratorResult** object. **IteratorResult** object has two properties value and done. The details of these properties are as follows: -

- The **value** property contains the current value for the iterator.
- The **done** property is Boolean type and represents whether Generator has fully completed.

In this chapter we have used a new NPM module called Babel CLI. This module comes with a new command line feature called **babel-node** to run babelified code.

> *You can get more information about the Babel CLI in the following URL: -*
>
> *http://babeljs.io/docs/usage/cli/*

Implementing Generators

ES6 provides Generators to create special type of function which can returns a series of values. The updated project **ES6FeatureDemo** structure look like following screenshot: -

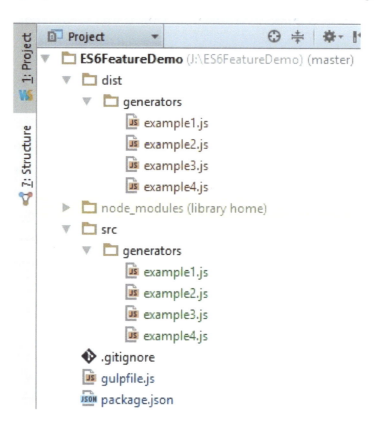

We have created a **generators** directory inside **src** folder to demonstrate ES6 Generator feature. The compiled code produced by Gulp task is present in **dist** folder in respective example files. Now we can develop some example to demonstrate generators.

Example: Declaring and Iterating Generator

The **src/generators/example1.js** file contains the code for defining a generator. The code content of **src/generators/example1.js** file are as follows: -

```javascript
//Iterating Generator
var FruitGenerator = function*(){
    yield "Apple";
    yield "Orange";
    yield "Grapes";
    yield "Mango";
};
var aFruitGenerator = FruitGenerator(),
    nextFruit = aFruitGenerator.next();
while(!nextFruit.done){
    console.log(nextFruit.value);
    nextFruit = aFruitGenerator.next();
}
```

In the previous code we have declared a simple generator function named **FruitGenerator**. This **FruitGenerator** has **yield** statements for fruits. A while loop is used to iterate over the iterator generated using **next()** method. Now we can run the **gulp** task to generate the babelified code. The code content of **dist/generators/example1.js** file are as follows: -

```javascript
"use strict";
//Iterating Generator
var FruitGenerator = regeneratorRuntime.mark(function FruitGenerator() {
    return regeneratorRuntime.wrap(function FruitGenerator$(_context) {
        while (1) {
            switch (_context.prev = _context.next) {
                case 0:
                    _context.next = 2;
                    return "Apple";
                case 2:
                    _context.next = 4;
                    return "Orange";
                case 4:
                    _context.next = 6;
                    return "Grapes";
                case 6:
                    _context.next = 8;
                    return "Mango";
                case 8:
                case "end":
                    return _context.stop();
            }
        }
    }, FruitGenerator, this);
});
var aFruitGenerator = FruitGenerator(),
```

```
      nextFruit = aFruitGenerator.next();
  while (!nextFruit.done) {
    console.log(nextFruit.value);
    nextFruit = aFruitGenerator.next();
  }
```

From the previous code we can observe that Babel has compiled the code to generate the supported javascript code. Now we can run **dist/generators/example1.js** code using **babel-node dist/generators/example1.js** command. The following screenshot shows the terminal with node execution and output in terminal: -

```
Terminal                                                    ✱ ▾  ↓

+  J:\ES6FeatureDemo>babel-node dist/generators/example1.js
✕  Apple
   Orange
   Grapes
   Mango


   J:\ES6FeatureDemo>▊
```

Example: Combine multiple generator

The yield keyword has another form and it is called as **yield with star * operator(yield*)**. This **yield*** operator can be used to call Generator inside a Generator. It means we can combine multiple Generators. The **src/generators/example2.js** file contains the code for combining multiple generators. The code content of **src/generators/example2.js** file are as follows: -

```
//Combining multiple generator
var FruitGenerator = function*(){
  yield "Apple";
  yield "Orange";
  yield "Grapes";
  yield "Mango";
};
var VegetableGenerator = function*(){
  yield "Potato";
  yield "Carrot";
  yield "tomato";
  yield "beetroot";
};
var FoodGenerator = function*(){
  yield "rice";
  yield* FruitGenerator();
  yield "Wheat";
  yield* VegetableGenerator();
```

```
        }
    var aFoodGenerator = FoodGenerator(),
        nextFood = aFoodGenerator.next();
    //next object  has value and done property
    console.log(JSON.stringify(nextFood));
    while(!nextFood.done){
        console.log(nextFood.value);
        nextFood = aFoodGenerator.next();
    }
```

In the previous code we have created 3 generators **FruitGenerator**, **VegetableGenerator** and **FoodGenerator**. The FruitGenerator returns different fruit names using yield keyword. VegetableGenerator returns different vegetable name using yield keyword.

The **FoodGenerator** returns food names like rice, wheat and also includes the **FruitGenerator** and **VegetableGenerator** items using **yield*** keyword. Now we can run the **gulp** task to generate the babelified code. The code content of **dist/generators/example2.js** file are as follows: -

```
"use strict";
//Combining multiple generator
var FruitGenerator = regeneratorRuntime.mark(function FruitGenerator() {
    return regeneratorRuntime.wrap(function FruitGenerator$(_context) {
        while (1) {
            switch (_context.prev = _context.next) {
                case 0:
                    _context.next = 2;
                    return "Apple";
                case 2:
                    _context.next = 4;
                    return "Orange";
                case 4:
                    _context.next = 6;
                    return "Grapes";
                case 6:
                    _context.next = 8;
                    return "Mango";
                case 8:
                case "end":
                    return _context.stop();
            }
        }
    }, FruitGenerator, this);
});
var VegetableGenerator = regeneratorRuntime.mark(function
VegetableGenerator() {
    return regeneratorRuntime.wrap(function VegetableGenerator$(_context2) {
        while (1) {
            switch (_context2.prev = _context2.next) {
```

```
            case 0:
                _context2.next = 2;
                return "Potato";
            case 2:
                _context2.next = 4;
                return "Carrot";
            case 4:
                _context2.next = 6;
                return "tomato";
            case 6:
                _context2.next = 8;
                return "beetroot";
            case 8:
            case "end":
                return _context2.stop();
            }
        }
    }, VegetableGenerator, this);
});
var FoodGenerator = regeneratorRuntime.mark(function FoodGenerator() {
    return regeneratorRuntime.wrap(function FoodGenerator$(_context3) {
        while (1) {
            switch (_context3.prev = _context3.next) {
            case 0:
                _context3.next = 2;
                return "rice";
            case 2:
                return _context3.delegateYield(FruitGenerator(), "t0", 3);
            case 3:
                _context3.next = 5;
                return "Wheat";

            case 5:
                return _context3.delegateYield(VegetableGenerator(), "t1", 6);
            case 6:
            case "end":
                return _context3.stop();
            }
        }
    }, FoodGenerator, this);
});
var aFoodGenerator = FoodGenerator(),
    nextFood = aFoodGenerator.next();
//next object  has value and done property
console.log(JSON.stringify(nextFood));
while (!nextFood.done) {
    console.log(nextFood.value);
    nextFood = aFoodGenerator.next();
}
```

From the previous code we can observe that Babel has compiled the code to generate the supported javascript code. Now we can run **dist/generators/example2.js** code using **babel-node dist/generators/example2.js** command. The following screenshot shows the terminal with node execution and output in terminal: -

```
Terminal                                                          ⚙ ↓
+  J:\ES6FeatureDemo>babel-node dist/generators/example2.js
✕  {"value":"rice","done":false}
   rice
   Apple
   Orange
   Grapes
   Mango
   Wheat           ▌
   Potato
   Carrot
   tomato
   beetroot

   J:\ES6FeatureDemo>
```

Example: Passing parameter to generator

This example is all about calculating whole square using algebraic elementary formula. The following image shows the formula for calculating whole square: -

$$(A + B)^2 = A^2 + B^2 + 2AB$$

The **src/generators/example3.js** file contains the code for passing parameter to Generator function. The code content of **src/generators/example3.js** file are as follows: -

```javascript
//Passing parameter to generator
var WholeSquareGenerator = function*(number){
  var a= 1 * (yield number),
     b= yield number;
  return (Math.pow(a,2)+Math.pow(b,2)+2*a*b);
};
// a=2, b=3 => a+b = 5 => result = 25
var squareGenerator = WholeSquareGenerator(1),
  yieldResult1 = squareGenerator.next(),
  yieldResult2 = squareGenerator.next(2),
  result = squareGenerator.next(3);
console.log("Last result return: ",result);
```

The preceding code contains a generator named **WholeSquareGenerator** which takes a number as input. This **WholeSquareGenerator** is used to calculate the **whole square** of **a+b** is equal to square $a^2 + b^2 + 2ab$. The preceding code takes **a=2** and **b=3** to calculate the whole square and prints the result **25** in the console. Now we can run the **gulp** task to generate the babelified code. The code content of **dist/generators/example3.js** file are as follows: -

```javascript
"use strict";
//Passing parameter to generator
var WholeSquareGenerator = regeneratorRuntime.mark(function
WholeSquareGenerator(number) {
  var a, b;
  return regeneratorRuntime.wrap(function WholeSquareGenerator$(_context)
{
    while (1) {
      switch (_context.prev = _context.next) {
        case 0:
          _context.next = 2;
          return number;
        case 2:
          _context.t0 = _context.sent;
          a = 1 * _context.t0;
          _context.next = 6;
          return number;
        case 6:
          b = _context.sent;
          return _context.abrupt(
                    "return", Math.pow(a, 2) +
                    Math.pow(b, 2) + 2 * a * b);
        case 8:
        case "end":
          return _context.stop();
      }
    }
  }, WholeSquareGenerator, this);
});
// a=2, b=3 => a+b = 5 => result = 25
var squareGenerator = WholeSquareGenerator(1),
  yieldResult1 = squareGenerator.next(),
  yieldResult2 = squareGenerator.next(2),
  result = squareGenerator.next(3);
console.log("Last result return: ", result);
```

From the previous code we can observe that Babel has compiled the code to generate the supported javascript code. Now we can run **dist/generators/example3.js** code using **babel-**

node dist/generators/example3.js command. The following screenshot shows the terminal with node execution and output in terminal: -

```
Terminal                                                    ⚙ ↓
+  J:\ES6FeatureDemo>babel-node dist/generators/example3.js
X  Last result return:  { value: 25, done: true }

   J:\ES6FeatureDemo>
```

Example: Dynamic generator creation

The **next()** method is used for iterating over a Generators. We can also iterate the Generator using **for...of** loop. Each iterated object in this loop is the value of **yield** statement. The **next()** method return an object with value and done property but in **for...of** loop each object is the direct value. The **src/generators/example4.js** file contains the code for creating generator dynamically. The code content of **src/generators/example4.js** file are as follows: -

```javascript
//Dynamic generator creation
var FruitGenerator = function*(){
    yield "Apple";
    yield "Orange";
    yield "Grapes";
    yield "Mango";
};
var fruitList = FruitGenerator();
for(var fruit of fruitList){
    console.log(fruit);
}
var createGenerator = function(itemArray){
    return function*(){
        for(var item of itemArray){
            yield item;
        }
    }();
};
var flowerArray= ["Rose","Lotus","Jasmine"],
    flowerList = createGenerator(flowerArray);
for(var flower of flowerList){
    console.log(flower);
}
```

The preceding code also contains a method **createGenerator()** which takes an **array** of item as input parameters and returns an **self-invoking** anonymous Generator function. The preceding code also contains a **FruitGenerator** with some yield statement with fruit names.

This **FruitGenerator** is then iterate using **for...of** loop and displayed in the browser. Now we can run the **gulp** task to generate the babelified code. The code content of **dist/generators/example4.js** file are as follows: -

```javascript
"use strict";
//Dynamic generator creation
var FruitGenerator = regeneratorRuntime.mark(function FruitGenerator() {
    return regeneratorRuntime.wrap(function FruitGenerator$(_context) {
        while (1) {
            switch (_context.prev = _context.next) {
                case 0:
                    _context.next = 2;
                    return "Apple";
                case 2:
                    _context.next = 4;
                    return "Orange";
                case 4:
                    _context.next = 6;
                    return "Grapes";
                case 6:
                    _context.next = 8;
                    return "Mango";
                case 8:
                case "end":
                    return _context.stop();
            }
        }
    }, FruitGenerator, this);
});
var fruitList = FruitGenerator();
var _iteratorNormalCompletion = true;
var _didIteratorError = false;
var _iteratorError = undefined;
try {
    for (var _iterator = fruitList[Symbol.iterator](), _step;
    !(_iteratorNormalCompletion = (_step = _iterator.next()).done);
    _iteratorNormalCompletion = true) {
        var fruit = _step.value;
        console.log(fruit);
    }
} catch (err) {
    _didIteratorError = true;
    _iteratorError = err;
} finally {
    try {
        if (!_iteratorNormalCompletion && _iterator.return) {
            _iterator.return();
        }
    } finally {
```

```
      if (_didIteratorError) {
        throw _iteratorError;
      }
    }
  }
}
var createGenerator = function createGenerator(itemArray) {
  return regeneratorRuntime.mark(function _callee() {
    var _iteratorNormalCompletion2, _didIteratorError2, _iteratorError2,
_iterator2, _step2, item;
    return regeneratorRuntime.wrap(function _callee$(_context2) {
      while (1) {
        switch (_context2.prev = _context2.next) {
          case 0:
            _iteratorNormalCompletion2 = true;
            _didIteratorError2 = false;
            _iteratorError2 = undefined;
            _context2.prev = 3;
            _iterator2 = itemArray[Symbol.iterator]();
          case 5:
            if (_iteratorNormalCompletion2 =
              (_step2 = _iterator2.next()).done) {
              _context2.next = 12;
              break;
            }
            item = _step2.value;
            _context2.next = 9;
            return item;
          case 9:
            _iteratorNormalCompletion2 = true;
            _context2.next = 5;
            break;
          case 12:
            _context2.next = 18;
            break;
          case 14:
            _context2.prev = 14;
            _context2.t0 = _context2["catch"](3);
            _didIteratorError2 = true;
            _iteratorError2 = _context2.t0;
          case 18:
            _context2.prev = 18;
            _context2.prev = 19;
            if (!_iteratorNormalCompletion2 && _iterator2.return) {
              _iterator2.return();
            }
          case 21:
            _context2.prev = 21;
            if (!_didIteratorError2) {
              _context2.next = 24;
```

```
                break;
            }
          throw _iteratorError2;
        case 24:
          return _context2.finish(21);
        case 25:
          return _context2.finish(18);
        case 26:
        case "end":
          return _context2.stop();
      }
    }
  }, _callee, this, [[3, 14, 18, 26], [19,, 21, 25]]);
  })();
};
var flowerArray = ["Rose", "Lotus", "Jasmine"],
  flowerList = createGenerator(flowerArray);
var _iteratorNormalCompletion3 = true;
var _didIteratorError3 = false;
var _iteratorError3 = undefined;
try {
  for (var _iterator3 = flowerList[Symbol.iterator](), _step3;
!(_iteratorNormalCompletion3 = (_step3 = _iterator3.next()).done);
_iteratorNormalCompletion3 = true) {
    var flower = _step3.value;
    console.log(flower);
  }
} catch (err) {
  _didIteratorError3 = true;
  _iteratorError3 = err;
} finally {
  try {
    if (!_iteratorNormalCompletion3 && _iterator3.return) {
      _iterator3.return();
    }
  } finally {
    if (_didIteratorError3) {
      throw _iteratorError3;
    }
  }
}
```

From the previous code we can observe that Babel has compiled the code to generate the supported javascript code. Now we can run **dist/generators/example4.js** code using **babel-node dist/generators/example4.js** command. The following screenshot shows the terminal with node execution and output in terminal: -

```
Terminal                                              ⚙ ⬇
+ J:\ES6FeatureDemo>babel-node dist/generators/example4.js
✗ Apple
  Orange
  Grapes
  Mango
  Rose
  Lotus
  Jasmine

  J:\ES6FeatureDemo>
```

Summary

In this chapter we have learnt about Symbols. We have also explored defining hidden property for an object with coded example. In the next chapter we will learn more ES6 features. Till then stay tuned.

About The Author

Sandeep Kumar Patel is a senior web developer and founder of www.tutorialsavvy.com, a widely- read programming blog since 2012. He has more than five years of experience in object-oriented JavaScript and JSON-based web applications development. He is GATE-2005 Information Technology (IT) qualified and has a Master's degree from VIT University, Vellore.

You can know more about him from his

- LinkedIn profile (http://www.linkedin.com/in/techblogger).
- He has received the Dzone Most Valuable Blogger (MVB) award for technical publications related to web technologies. His article can be viewed at http://www.dzone.com/users/sandeepgiet.
- He has also received the Java Code Geek (JCG) badge for a technical article published in JCG. His article can be viewed at http://www.javacodegeeks.com/author/sandeep-kumar-patel/.

- Author of "Instant GSON" for Packt publication, http://www.packtpub.com/create-json-data-java-objects-implement-with-gson-library/book

Questions or comments? E-mail me at sandeeppateltech@gmail.com or find me on the following social networks:-

- Facebook Page: http://www.facebook.com/SandeepTechTutorials .

- Tutorial Blog: http://www.tutorialsavvy.com

One Last Thing...

When you turn the page, Kindle will give you the opportunity to rate this book and share your thoughts on Facebook and Twitter. If you believe the book is worth sharing, please would you take a few seconds to let your friends know about it? If it turns out to make a difference in their professional lives, they'll be forever grateful to you, as will I.

All the best,

Sandeep Kumar Patel.